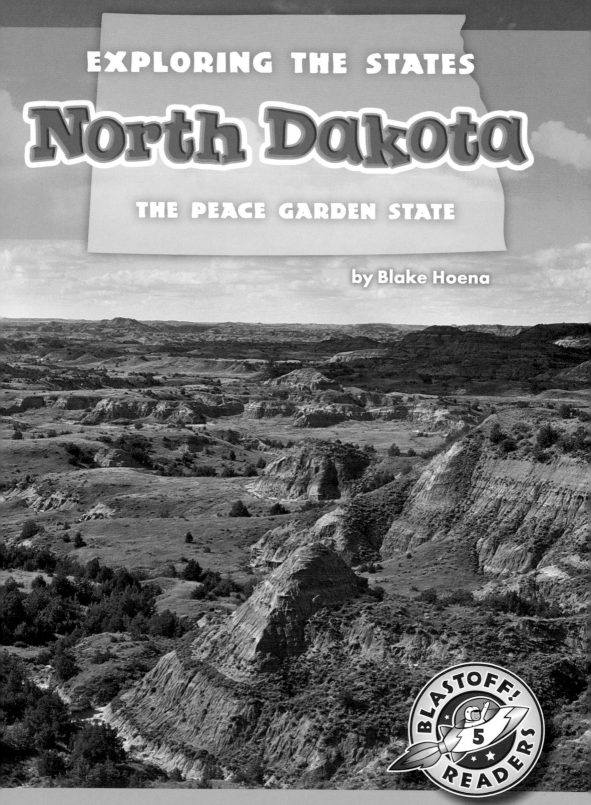

EXPLORING THE STATES

North Dakota

THE PEACE GARDEN STATE

by Blake Hoena

BLASTOFF!
5
READERS

BELLWETHER MEDIA · MINNEAPOLIS, MN

Note to Librarians, Teachers, and Parents:

Blastoff! Readers are carefully developed by literacy experts and combine standards-based content with developmentally appropriate text.

Level 1 provides the most support through repetition of high-frequency words, light text, predictable sentence patterns, and strong visual support.

Level 2 offers early readers a bit more challenge through varied simple sentences, increased text load, and less repetition of high-frequency words.

Level 3 advances early-fluent readers toward fluency through increased text and concept load, less reliance on visuals, longer sentences, and more literary language.

Level 4 builds reading stamina by providing more text per page, increased use of punctuation, greater variation in sentence patterns, and increasingly challenging vocabulary.

Level 5 encourages children to move from "learning to read" to "reading to learn" by providing even more text, varied writing styles, and less familiar topics.

Whichever book is right for your reader, Blastoff! Readers are the perfect books to build confidence and encourage a love of reading that will last a lifetime!

This edition first published in 2014 by Bellwether Media, Inc.

No part of this publication may be reproduced in whole or in part without written permission of the publisher. For information regarding permission, write to Bellwether Media, Inc., Attention: Permissions Department, 5357 Penn Avenue South, Minneapolis, MN 55419.

Library of Congress Cataloging-in-Publication Data

Hoena, B. A.
  North Dakota / by Blake Hoena.
     p. cm. – (Blastoff! readers. Exploring the states)
  Includes bibliographical references and index.
  Summary: "Developed by literacy experts for students in grades three through seven, this book introduces young readers to the geography and culture of North Dakota"–Provided by publisher.
  ISBN 978-1-62617-033-9 (hardcover : alk. paper)
  1. North Dakota–Juvenile literature. I. Title.
  F636.3.H64 2014
  978.4–dc23
                                                                      2013008949

Printed in the United States of America, North Mankato, MN.

Table of Contents

Where Is North Dakota?

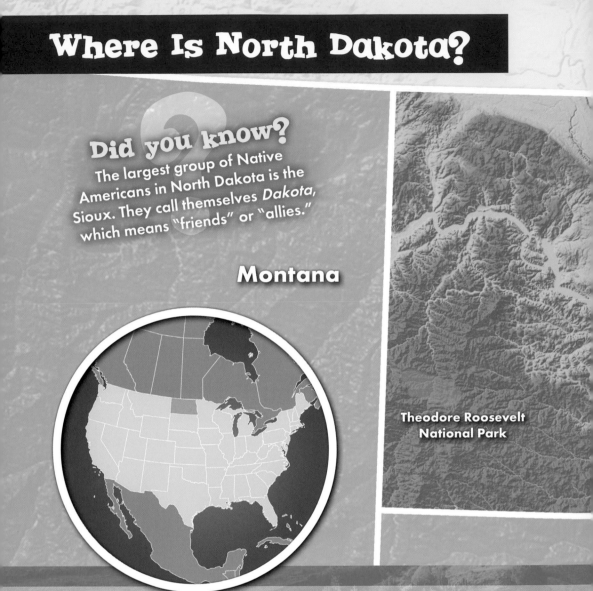

Did you know?
The largest group of Native Americans in North Dakota is the Sioux. They call themselves *Dakota*, which means "friends" or "allies."

Montana

Theodore Roosevelt National Park

North Dakota is a **Midwestern** state that sits right below Canada. The Red River forms its ragged eastern border with Minnesota. Montana lies to the west. Its southern neighbor is South Dakota.

Canada

N
W   E
S

Minot

Minnesota

Grand Forks

North Dakota

Red River

Fargo

★ Bismarck

South Dakota

North Dakota is a fairly large state. However, it is one of the least populated. Its capital city of Bismarck is home to only 61,272 people. Fargo is the state's largest city. It sits in the Red River Valley near the Minnesota border.

Native peoples have been living in North Dakota for thousands of years. Sioux and Ojibwe hunted the bison that roamed the area in large herds. The first Europeans arrived in the 1700s. By 1818, the United States controlled all the land that makes up North Dakota.

bison hunt

North Dakota Timeline!

1738: Pierre Gaultier de Varennes is perhaps the first European to explore North Dakota.

1861: Congress creates the Dakota Territory.

1863: The U.S. government opens the Dakota Territory to white settlers.

1871: The city of Fargo is founded.

1881: Sioux leader Sitting Bull surrenders to U.S. troops after almost twenty years of fighting.

1889: North Dakota becomes the thirty-ninth state.

1947: Theodore Roosevelt National Park is established.

1956: The Garrison Dam starts producing electricity.

2000s: An oil mining boom begins in western North Dakota.

oil mining

Theodore Roosevelt National Park

Sitting Bull

The Land

North Dakota has three main regions. The Red River Valley runs along the state's eastern edge. Thousands of years ago, a lake covered this area. When it dried up, the soil that was left behind created **fertile** farmland.

The Drift **Prairie** lies in the center of the state. Long ago, **glaciers** left rich soil in this area of gently rolling hills. The **Great Plains** spread across the state's southwestern half. This region is mostly flat, except where the Missouri River has carved out valleys. North Dakota has harsh, cold winters and hot, sticky summers.

Did you know?

The Great Plains extend into ten U.S. states. They reach west to the Rocky Mountains and south to Texas.

North Dakota's Climate

average °F

spring
Low: 31°
High: 54°

summer
Low: 55°
High: 81°

fall
Low: 31°
High: 55°

winter
Low: 3°
High: 23°

The Badlands

Theodore Roosevelt
National Park

Tucked into North Dakota's southwestern corner is an area known as the Badlands. It earned this name because of its dry, rocky slopes and harsh, windy weather. Both Native Americans and European explorers considered the area a difficult land to cross.

Today, people admire the Badlands for its spectacular scenery. Over thousands of years, wind and rain have worn away soil and rock. This has left behind deep **gullies**, steep **ravines**, and oddly shaped rock formations. The **erosion** has also exposed colorful layers of rock. Each of these layers was formed during a different era in Earth's history.

ginko leaf fossil

fun fact

The Badlands contain one of the world's largest deposits of fossils. The ancient remains of many plants and animals can be found there.

Wildlife

North Dakota is mostly prairie. In some areas, grasslands stretch as far as the eye can see. Wild roses, black-eyed Susans, and other colorful wildflowers bloom throughout much of the state.

Wetlands in the Drift Prairie are perfect nesting stops for **migrating** birds. Canada geese, sandhill cranes, and all kinds of ducks fly across North Dakota's skies. Large animals such as elk, bison, and moose roam the wilderness. The state is also home to beavers, prairie dogs, and other small animals.

flickertail ground squirrel

fun fact

Pelicans are not just ocean birds. More than 10,000 white pelicans nest at the Chase Lake National Wildlife Refuge outside of Medina.

white pelican

bison

13

International Peace Garden

North Dakota is called the Peace Garden State. It earned this nickname from the International Peace Garden, which straddles the U.S.-Canada border. The park is a sign of friendship between the two countries.

Fort Mandan

Many landmarks in North Dakota celebrate the state's past. A trading center for Native Americans once stood along the Knife River. Now its remains are preserved in a National Historic Site. In the early 1800s, Meriwether Lewis and William Clark passed through the state during their journey to the West. Today, visitors can tour a **replica** of Fort Mandan, where the explorers survived a North Dakota winter.

The city of Fargo sits along the border with Minnesota. It is home to about 100,000 people. Early settlers were drawn to the area because of its rich farmland. The city was also an important stop for **steamboats** traveling along the Red River.

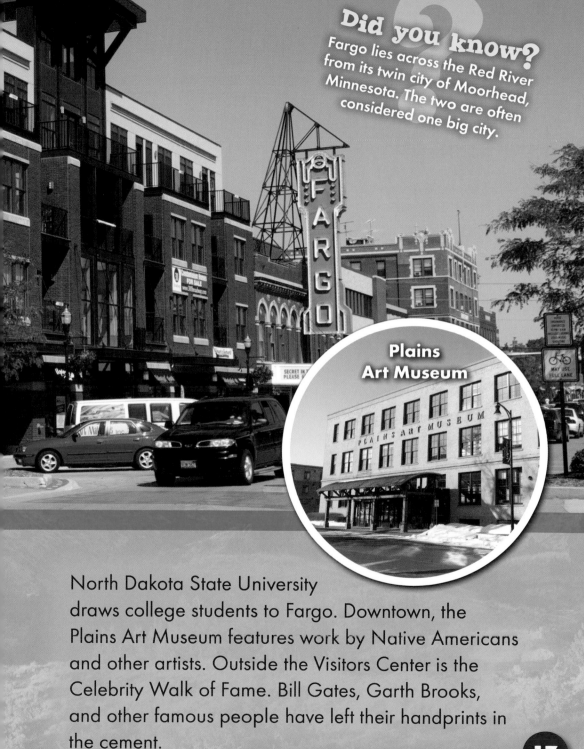

Did you know?
Fargo lies across the Red River from its twin city of Moorhead, Minnesota. The two are often considered one big city.

Plains Art Museum

North Dakota State University draws college students to Fargo. Downtown, the Plains Art Museum features work by Native Americans and other artists. Outside the Visitors Center is the Celebrity Walk of Fame. Bill Gates, Garth Brooks, and other famous people have left their handprints in the cement.

Mining is a big business in North Dakota. The state holds large amounts of coal. In recent years, oil and natural gas have become more important. In the early 2000s, new technology allowed companies to mine oil in the western part of the state. Thousands of people have moved to the area for work.

Farming is also important to North Dakota. The state's vast grasslands are perfect for grazing cattle. North Dakota farmers are leaders in the production of wheat, barley, sunflower seeds, and honey. Many North Dakotans work in factories that process the state's farm products. Others have **service jobs** at restaurants that serve the farm food.

Where People Work in North Dakota

manufacturing
6%

farming and
natural resources
9%

government
16%

services
69%

Playing

North Dakotans like to play outside. During the warmer months, they mountain bike and hike on state trails. When the snow falls, they **snowmobile** and cross-country ski. Hunters target pheasants, deer, and other **game**. Fishers cast lines for walleye and northern pike. Bird-watchers enjoy the flocks of waterbirds that nest in the wetlands.

cornfield maze

Farmers sometimes turn their work into play. They carve mazes out of cornfields and let people find their way through. They invite friends for bumpy hayrides pulled by tractors. At **threshing** parties, everybody helps with the wheat harvest.

Scandinavian Lefse

Ingredients:

- 3 cups cooled mashed potatoes (instant are okay)
- 3 cups sifted flour
- 1 teaspoon salt
- 1 tablespoon sugar
- 2 tablespoons butter (melted)
- 2 tablespoons cream or half & half

Directions:

1. Mix all ingredients in a large bowl.

2. Drop one tablespoon of dough at a time onto a floured surface. Roll out until thin.

3. On a preheated griddle, cook on both sides. Cook until a few light brown spots appear. Cool on dish towels.

4. To serve, spread with butter, sprinkle with sugar and cinnamon, and roll up.

borscht

chokecherries

! **fun fact**

North Dakota's state fruit is the chokecherry. These small berries can be used to flavor butter and jelly. They also add a sweet tang to barbecue sauce.

Native Americans and early explorers relied on bison for food. Long ago, massive herds of these giant animals roamed the plains. These days, bison are raised by farmers. Their meat is made into burgers, steaks, chili, and meatloaf. Hunters also bring home game birds and **venison** to cook.

North Dakota recipes represent the heritage of those who live there. People combine beets and other vegetables to make *borscht*. German-Russians brought this bright red soup to North Dakota in the late 1800s. North Dakotans with **Scandinavian** roots enjoy *lefse*. These thin potato cakes are popular during the holidays.

**United Tribes
International Powwow**

North Dakotans hold many festivals that celebrate their roots. The Killdeer Mountain Roundup **Rodeo** is one of the oldest rodeos in North Dakota. Thousands come to watch cowboys and cowgirls compete in riding contests. Minot hosts Norsk Høstfest in the fall. People honor their Scandinavian heritage with music, dancing, and more.

Norsk Høstfest

Several Native American **powwows** are held throughout the state. One of the largest is the United Tribes International Powwow in Bismarck. Visitors come to see more than 1,500 dancers and drummers perform.

German-Russians

Many German farmers moved to Russia in the late 1700s. However, Russian laws kept them from expressing their heritage. In the late 1800s, many Germans fled to the United States in search of freedom.

These German-Russians settled throughout the Great Plains, including south-central North Dakota. Today, their **descendants** celebrate their roots with special foods. *Knoephla* is a creamy potato and dumpling soup. *Kuchen* is a type of fruit-filled pastry. The German-Russian settlers are remembered for their hard work. They helped form the strong farming community that defines North Dakota today.

kuchen

settling the Great Plains

Fast Facts
About North Dakota

North Dakota's Flag

North Dakota's flag has a dark blue background and a bald eagle in the center. The eagle grasps an olive branch in one talon and arrows in the other. In its beak, the eagle holds a ribbon that says, "*E Pluribus Unum,*" or "Out of Many, One." The 13 stars above the eagle represent the 13 original states.

State Flower
wild prairie rose

State Nicknames:	The Peace Garden State The Sioux State The Flickertail State
State Motto:	"Liberty and Union, Now and Forever, One and Inseparable"
Year of Statehood:	1889
Capital City:	Bismarck
Other Major Cities:	Fargo, Grand Forks, Minot
Population:	672,591 (2010)
Area:	70,698 square miles (183,107 square kilometers); North Dakota is the 19th largest state.
Major Industries:	mining, farming
Natural Resources:	soil, oil, coal, natural gas
State Government:	94 representatives; 47 senators
Federal Government:	1 representative; 2 senators
Electoral Votes:	3

State Bird
western meadowlark

State Animal
northern pike

Glossary

descendants—people who come from a common ancestor

erosion—the slow wearing away of soil by water or wind

fertile—able to support growth

game—wild animals hunted for food or sport

glaciers—massive sheets of ice that cover large areas of land

Great Plains—a region of flat or gently rolling land in the central United States; the Great Plains stretch over about one-third of the country.

gullies—large ditches

Midwestern—belonging to a region of 12 states in the north-central United States

migrating—traveling from one place to another, often with the seasons

native—originally from a specific place

powwows—celebrations of Native American culture that often include singing and dancing

prairie—a large area of level or rolling grassland

ravines—deep, narrow valleys

replica—an exact copy

rodeo—an event where people compete at tasks such as bull riding and calf roping; cowboys once completed these tasks as part of their daily work.

Scandinavian—from Norway, Denmark, or Sweden

service jobs—jobs that perform tasks for people or businesses

snowmobile—to drive a vehicle that is made to move quickly over snow

steamboats—boats powered by steam

threshing—separating the seeds or grains from the rest of a plant

venison—deer meat

To Learn More

AT THE LIBRARY
Dwyer, Helen. *Sioux History and Culture.*
New York, N.Y.: Garth Stevens Pub., 2012.

Murray, Julie. *North Dakota*. Minneapolis, Minn.:
ABDO Pub. Co., 2012.

Watson, Galadriel Findlay. *North Dakota: The
Peace Garden State*. New York, N.Y.: Weigl, 2012.

ON THE WEB
Learning more about North Dakota
is as easy as 1, 2, 3.

1. Go to www.factsurfer.com.

2. Enter "North Dakota" into the search box.

3. Click the "Surf" button and you will see a list of
   related Web sites.

With factsurfer.com, finding more information is just
a click away.

Index